WHIPPET

BACK
Broad and well muscled

STERN
Low with upward curve

HINDQUARTERS
Long and powerful

FEET
Well formed with hard,
thick pads

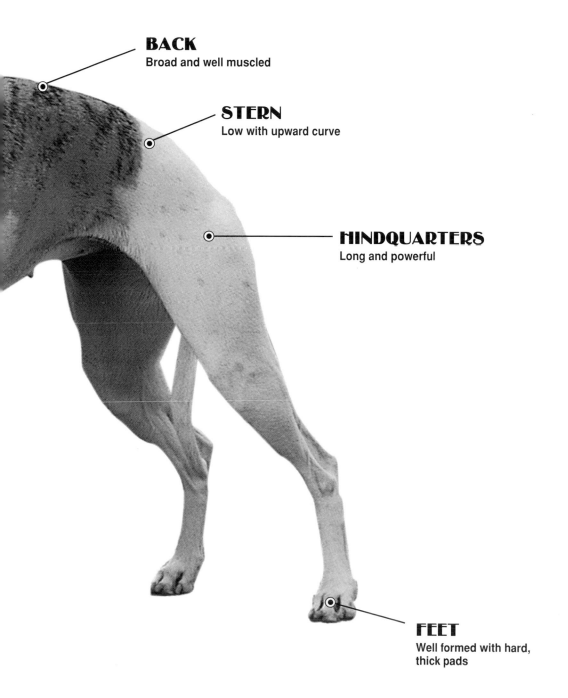

Title Page: Whippet photographed by Isabelle Francais

Photographers: Isabelle Francais, Pets by Paulette, Ron Reagan, Karen Taylor, Adrien Tudor

Distributed in the UNITED STATES to the Pet Trade by T.F.H. Publications, Inc., 1 TFH Plaza, Neptune City, NJ 07753; on the Internet at www.tfh.com; in CANADA by Rolf C. Hagen Inc., 3225 Sartelon St., Montreal, Quebec H4R 1E8; Pet Trade by H & L Pet Supplies Inc., 27 Kingston Crescent, Kitchener, Ontario N2B 2T6; in ENGLAND by T.F.H. Publications, PO Box 74, Havant PO9 5TT; in AUSTRALIA AND THE SOUTH PACIFIC by T.F.H. (Australia), Pty. Ltd., Box 149, Brookvale 2100 N.S.W., Australia; in NEW ZEALAND by Brooklands Aquarium Ltd., 5 McGiven Drive, New Plymouth, RD1 New Zealand; in SOUTH AFRICA by Rolf C. Hagen S.A. (PTY.) LTD., P.O. Box 201199, Durban North 4016, South Africa; in JAPAN by T.F.H. Publications, Japan—Jiro Tsuda, 10-12-3 Ohjidai, Sakura, Chiba 285, Japan. Published by T.F.H. Publications, Inc.
MANUFACTURED IN THE
UNITED STATES OF AMERICA
BY T.F.H. PUBLICATIONS, INC.

WHIPPET

A COMPLETE AND RELIABLE HANDBOOK

Dean Keppler

RX-138

CONTENTS

HISTORY AND ORIGIN OF THE WHIPPET

The facts surrounding the true origin of the Whippet breed are both controversial and unclear. Despite varied opinions among breeders and dog fanciers, a few plausible theories have continued to hold their own throughout time. Evidence has proven that this sleek, athletic, short-haired, compact breed has most likely derived from other Greyhound-like sighthounds similar in appearance. Artwork frequently presented during the Middle Ages and the Renaissance often portrayed dogs closely resembling today's Whippet. It wasn't until the mid-1800s in the industrial areas of Northern England that the Whippet's popularity began to grow.

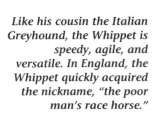

Like his cousin the Italian Greyhound, the Whippet is speedy, agile, and versatile. In England, the Whippet quickly acquired the nickname, "the poor man's race horse."

Prized for their brilliant speed and versatility, these little Greyhound-like dogs were often raced in the fields, meadows, and roadways by the blue-collar workers of England. Whippet racing became so popular that they quickly acquired the nicknames "the poor man's race horse" or "the poor man's race dog."

Opposite: The Whippet's origin is unclear, although there is proven evidence that the breed derived from other Greyhound-like sighthounds similar in appearance.

The Whippet's first introduction in the United States dates back to before 1900, but it wasn't until the 1930s that the American Kennel Club (AKC) finally recognized the breed. Early records dated in 1876 also indicate that the first Whippets were show dogs, but long before the breed gained popularity in the show ring, their superior ability for hunting small game was widely recognized. The Whippet quickly became the perfect type of dog for hunting and coursing rabbits in the open field. The early Whippet's combination of strength, speed, elegance, and intelligence crossed with other breeds' characteristics certainly explains its incredible sturdiness as a breed today.

In 1899, the Whippet Club, which is the parent club of the breed, was first formed to promote a fundamental standard for the breed. Several kennels were responsible for the breed's development over the years, but two of the most influential include Albert Lamotte's Shirley Kennel and the Bottomley brothers' Manorley Kennels.

Considered a sturdy breed, the Whippet has a brilliant combination of strength and grace. Here, these Whippets get ready for a day of lure coursing.

Once completing his championship in 1902, Lamotte's Ch. Shirley Wanderer went on to become one of the first dominant stud dogs for the breed. Wanderer's son, Ch. Manorley Maori, also became an influential champion, producing many winning offspring. Although the Whippet was first officially recognized in the US and not in England, several famous Whippets have British-oriented pedigrees.

Bay View Kennel, established in 1903, was the first existing Whippet kennel and is recorded as the first breeders of an American Whippet champion, named Bay View Pride. In fact, Bay View, operated by Karl Bjurman, was responsible for more than half of the first dozen American Whippet champions. Since the early 1900s, the number of Whippet breeders has grown tremendously. Some of the most dominant kennels that have had the greatest impact on the breed include Meander, Mardormere, Stoney Meadows, Pennyworth, Whipporwill, and Sporting Fields to name just a few. Most Whippet pedigrees can be traced to one or more of the above kennels.

Before the Whippet became a popular show dog, he was a prized hunting dog, known for expertly locating and coursing rabbits in the open field.

CHARACTERISTICS OF THE WHIPPET

WHY A WHIPPET?

The Whippet has so many positive attributes that it is often difficult to describe them all in a few sentences or even a few paragraphs for that matter. Their smooth, elegant, stylish appearance combined with their sweet temperament and eagerness to please makes them wonderful pets for both the young and old. Fiercely loyal and always willing to accommodate their master, Whippets make excellent family pets and love to participate in various leisure activities.

Although the Whippet is an energetic and athletic dog in the field, he is gentle and loving in a family environment and makes a wonderful housepet.

Whether it's going for a jog in the park, a spending a day at the dog show, or just watching some television, the Whippet makes for an unbeatable companion. Unfortunately, the Whippet's sleek appearance is sometimes deceiving to the beginner's eye and they are often classified as high-strung or nervous dogs, but the truth is just the opposite. The Whippet is a tremendous runner and athlete in the field, but extremely calm and gentle in the home.

Like most breeds, the Whippet adores human attention and is eager to please those that he is closest to. This little guy and his buddies look content lounging in the afternoon sun.

WHIPPETS AS PETS

Unlike some breeds, the Whippet thrives on human attention. They simply adore people but still manage to maintain their individuality and complete self-confidence. A devoted pet to his owner, the Whippet easily adjusts to the lifestyle provided for him, whether it's in an apartment, house, kennel, or farm setting. The Whippet's high level of tolerance and flexibility creates little or no problems under most types of housing conditions. Like most short-hair breeds, they cannot withstand the severe cold but will adjust accordingly to changing climates.

The Whippet's small-to-medium size and short coat makes him easy to groom and care for. As far as

Opposite: These three sighthound relatives—the Greyhound, the Whippet, and the Italian Greyhound—show of the beauty and spirit that embody these breeds.

health matters are concerned, the Whippet presents few problems and is mostly disease and injury resistant. The breed offers a variety of colors including blue, black, brindle, red, fawn, and many combinations thereof.

Perhaps one of the greatest attributes of the Whippet is their ability to perform multiple functions. They can be a wonderful family pet, a field and lure courser, a show dog, an obedience performer, or even a combination of the above. In field coursing, the Whippet, like his relative the Greyhound, runs down small game using his sight, agility, and incredible speed. Organized Whippet coursing continues to grow in popularity around the world, but has at times suffered minor setbacks due to protesters who believe that using live hare is morally wrong. Such protests make coursing using live game a somewhat controversial sport.

LURE COURSING

Lure coursing involves open-field coursing of an artificial electric lure. The Whippet is trained to chase a white bag attached to a line that is spread out over

These Whippets in action show the strength and agility prevalent in the breed.

a field and operated mechanically. The white bag is intended to imitate live game as it twists and turns at rapid speed. The American Kennel Club recently recognized lure coursing as a registered field trial event, and with a little luck and practice, your new Whippet could gain a lure coursing title. If nothing else, lure coursing provides excellent exercise for the Whippet and enables the dog to perform his original purpose of hunting and chasing live game.

WHIPPET RACING

Whippet racing was very popular in England during the 1920s and 1930s. Primitive Whippet racing during this era often involved a pack of Whippets that were

The Whippet is a born athlete, inbred with a love for running and competing. Whippet race meets are very popular events and take place all over the country.

let loose in an enclosed area used for running down rabbits, while onlookers wagered on which Whippet they believed would kill the rabbit first. Fortunately, Whippet racing grew to a more sophisticated level as competitive box racing on a racetrack was introduced. Today, the American Whippet Club sponsors Whippet racing as an amateur sport with the intention of improving Whippet breeding programs. Whippets that race competitively may earn the Award of Racing Merit title for successfully capturing the needed points that are awarded at each race meet. Whippet race

CHARACTERISTICS

If you are planning to show your Whippet competitively, be sure that you have the time, patience, and dedication required to compete successfully in the show ring.

meets take place in all different parts of the country, attracting over 1,000 entries each year. The Whippet's love for running and his competitive nature make him a natural at racing

WHIPPETS AS SHOW DOGS

There is nothing more fascinating and exciting than the sport of showing a dog. Whether your dog wins or loses, it is extremely gratifying to compete with fellow exhibitors in the show ring. Show preparation for both the owner and dog requires countless hours of hard work, training, and patience, as well as a little luck. Nonetheless, dog shows provide enjoyment for thousands of people from around the world that wish to participate and compete in this challenging and sometimes frustrating sport.

The main purpose of dog shows is to have the finest specimens of a breed presented in the best show condition possible. This includes proper lead breaking, diet, grooming, and the presentation of your dog known as "handling." Each of these factors are very important to your overall success in the show ring. During the judging procedure, the exhibitor will see how his or her dog compares to the ideal standard of

Opposite: The Whippet is an ideal show candidate because his coat does not require as much maintenance as a long-haired breed.

16

the breed based entirely on the judge's expert opinion. Unfortunately, no two judges ever interpret a dog's appearance the same way and any dog's success can vary from day to day, but that is what makes the game so suspenseful and enjoyable.

The Whippet is an excellent choice when it comes to the show ring, mainly because they don't require the intense grooming, clipping, and trimming that other long-coated breeds do. A quick bath before the show, a nall clipping, and simple hand grooming is all the preparation a Whippet needs. The Whippet's upbeat enthusiasm for just about everything and anybody also helps him to perform excellently. Although there's a lot to learn before one can compete successfully in dog shows, a well-trained Whippet is the best choice to start with.

WHIPPETS IN OBEDIENCE

The Whippets' loyalty to their owners and eagerness to please make them favorable obedience can-

In conformation competition, your Whippet will be judged on how closely he compares to the breed standard.

Showing off his agility, this Whippet makes it over the jump with ease and precision.

didates. Unlike some other sighthounds that are independent by nature, the Whippet's temperament allows for a close bonding between handler and dog. Whippets are now frequently competing in obedience trials across the country. The companion dog title, often referred to as CD, is the lowest obedience title offered by the American Kennel Club; however, several Whippets have earned their CDs and have even graduated to other higher obedience titles. Obedience training, like show training, requires long hours and hard work. Persistent training and positive reassurance is essential for successful obedience training. Once the Whippet has mastered the basic obedience commands of sit, stay, come, and heel, he may be used as a therapy dog for the handicapped and elderly.

STANDARD FOR THE WHIPPET

As you're probably well aware, each breed of dog has his or her own desirable characteristics. The official description of what the ideal specimen should look like is known as breed standard. The breed standard is important in helping both the novice and experienced dog owner recognize what their breed of dog should look like. For those involved in showing dogs, such as judges, breeders, and exhibitors, the standard is extremely important. Several different dog organizations worldwide recognize different standards. Over the years, the Whippet standard in both America and other countries has changed periodically.

The Whippet's appearance should be striking, conveying muscular strength, elegance, and a symmetrical outline.

The latest change to the American Kennel Club standard occurred in 1993. Previous changes to the standard occurred in 1976, 1971, and 1955. Over the years, the trend toward a more detailed and descriptive standard is evident.

OFFICIAL AKC STANDARD FOR THE WHIPPET

General Appearance

A medium size sighthound giving the appearance of elegance and fitness, denoting great speed, power, and balance without coarseness. A true sporting hound that covers a maximum of distance with a minimum of lost motion. Should convey an impression of beautifully balanced muscular power and strength, combined with great elegance and grace of outline. Symmetry of outline, muscular development, and powerful gait are the main considerations; the dog being built for speed and work, all forms of exaggeration should be avoided.

Size, Proportion, Substance

Ideal height for dogs, 19 to 22 inches; for bitches 18 to 21 inches, measured at the highest point of the withers. More than one-half inch above or below the stated limits will disqualify. Length from forechest to buttocks equal to or slightly greater than height at the withers. Moderate bone throughout.

According to the official standard for the Whippet, eyes should be large and dark, displaying a keen, intelligent expression.

Head

Keen intelligent alert expression. *Eyes* large and dark. Both eyes must be of the same color. Yellow or light eyes should be strictly penalized. Blue or wall eyes shall disqualify. Fully pigmented eyelids are desirable. Rose *ears*, small, fine in texture; in repose, thrown back and folded along neck. Fold should be maintained when at attention. Erect ears should be severely penalized. *Skull* long and lean, fairly wide between the ears, scarcely perceptible stop. *Muzzle* should be long and powerful, denoting great strength of bite, without coarseness. Lack of underjaw should be strictly penalized. Nose entirely black. *Teeth* of upper jaw should fit closely over teeth of lower jaw creating a scissors bite. Teeth should be white and strong. Undershot shall disqualify. Overshot one-quarter inch or more shall disqualify.

Neck, Topline, Body

Neck long, clean and muscular, well arched with no suggestion of throatiness, widening gracefully into the top of the shoulder. A short thick neck, or a ewe neck, should be penalized. The *back* is broad, firm and well muscled, having length over the loin. The backline runs smoothly from the withers with a graceful natural arch, not too accentuated, beginning over the loin and carrying through over the croup; the arch is continuous without flatness. A dip behind shoulder

Opposite: This Whippet displays his perfect form, complete with long shoulder blades, strong upper arms, and straight forelegs.

Defining the grace that characterizes this breed, a correctly formed Whippet should have a long, lean neck.

blades, wheelback, flat back or a steep or flat croup should be penalized. *Brisket* very deep, reaching as nearly as possible to the point of the elbow. *Ribs* well sprung but with no suggestion of barrel shape. The space between the forelegs is filled in so that there is no appearance of a hollow between them. There is a definite tuckup of the underline. The *tail* long and tapering, reaching to the hipbone when drawn through between the hind legs. When the dog is in motion, the tail is carried low with only a gentle upward curve; tail should not be carried higher than top of the back.

Forequarters

Shoulder blade long, well laid back, with flat muscles, allowing for moderate space between shoulder blades at peak of withers. Upper arm of equal length, placed so that the elbow falls directly under the withers. The points of the elbows should point neither in nor out, but straight back. A steep shoulder, short upper arm, a heavily muscled or loaded shoulder, or a very narrow shoulder, all of which restrict low free movement, should be strictly penalized. *Forelegs* straight, giving appearance of strength and substance of bone. Pas-

Although the color of the Whippet's coat is not important, the standard states that it should be short, close, smooth, and firm in texture. These two buddies proudly show off their well-groomed coats.

A Whippet's gait is low, fast, and smooth, giving the appearance of both elegance and fitness.

terns strong, slightly bent and flexible. Bowed legs, tied-in elbows, legs lacking substance, legs set far under the body so as to create an exaggerated forechest, weak or upright pasterns should be strictly penalized.

Both front and rear feet must be well formed with hard, thick pads. Feet more hare than cat, but both are acceptable. Flat, splayed or soft feet without thick hard pads should be strictly penalized. Toes should be long, close and well arched. Nails strong and naturally short or of moderate length. Dewclaws may be removed.

Hindquarters

Long and powerful. The thighs are broad and muscular, stifles well bent; muscles are long and flat and carry well down toward the hock. The hocks are well let down and close to the ground. Sickle or cow hocks should be strictly penalized.

Coat

Short, close, smooth and firm in texture. Any other coat shall be a disqualification. Old scars and injuries, the result of work or accident, should not be allowed to prejudice the dog's chance in the show ring.

Color

Color immaterial.

Gait

Low, free moving and smooth, with reach in the forequarters and strong drive in the hindquarters. The dog has great freedom of action when viewed from the side; the forelegs move forward close to the ground to give a long, low reach; the hind legs have strong propelling power.When moving and viewed from front or rear, legs should turn neither in nor out, nor should feet cross or interfere with each other. Lack of front reach or rear drive, or a short, hackney gait with high wrist action, should be strictly penalized. Crossing in front or moving too close should be strictly penalized.

Temperament

Amiable, friendly, gentle, but capable of great intensity during sporting pursuits.

DISQUALIFICATIONS

More than one-half inch above or below stated height limits. Blue or wall eyes. Undershot, overshot one-quarter inch or more. Any coat other than short, close, smooth and firm in texture.

Approved August 10, 1993
Effective September 29, 1993

Friendly and gentle, the Whippet makes for a wonderful companion and pet, as well as an energetic and intense competitor in the show ring.

YOUR PUPPY'S NEW HOME

Puppies depend on their mother for all of their basic needs, including food, comfort, and discipline.

Before actually collecting your puppy, it is better that you purchase the basic items you will need in advance of the pup's arrival date. This allows you more opportunity to shop around and ensure you have exactly what you want rather than having to buy lesser quality in a hurry.

It is always better to collect the puppy as early in the day as possible. In most instances this will mean that the puppy has a few hours with your family before it is time to retire for his first night's sleep away from his former home.

YOUR PUPPY'S NEW HOME

If the breeder is local, then you may not need any form of box to place the puppy in when you bring him home. A member of the family can hold the pup in his lap—duly protected by some towels just in case the puppy becomes car sick! Be sure to advise the breeder at what time you hope to arrive for the puppy, as this will obviously influence the feeding of the pup that morning or afternoon. If you arrive early in the day, then they will likely only give the pup a light breakfast so as to reduce the risk of travel sickness.

If the trip will be of a few hours duration, you should take a travel crate with you. The crate will provide your pup with a safe place to lie down and rest during the trip. During the trip, the puppy will no doubt wish to relieve his bowels, so you will have to make a few stops. On a long journey you may need a rest yourself, and can take the opportunity to let the puppy get some fresh air. However, do not let the puppy walk where there may have been a lot of other dogs because he might pick up an infection. Also, if he relieves his bowels at such a time, do not just leave the feces where they were dropped. This is the height of irre-

Opposite: It's up to you, the owner, to make sure that your new puppy has everything he needs to grow into a healthy and responsible adult.

It takes a lot of time for a new puppy to adjust to his surroundings, so allow him to get used to your family and home.

sponsibility. It has resulted in many public parks and other places actually banning dogs. You can purchase poop-scoops from your pet shop and should have them with you whenever you are taking the dog out where he might foul a public place.

Your journey home should be made as quickly as possible. If it is a hot day, be sure the car interior is amply supplied with fresh air. It should never be too hot or too cold for the puppy. The pup must never be placed where he might be subject to a draft. If the journey requires an overnight stop at a motel, be aware that other guests will not appreciate a puppy crying half the night. You must regard the puppy as a baby and comfort him so he does not cry for long periods. The worst thing you can do is to shout at or smack him. This will mean your relationship is off to a really bad start. You wouldn't smack a baby, and your puppy is still very much just this.

ON ARRIVING HOME

By the time you arrive home the puppy may be very tired, in which case he should be taken to his sleeping area and allowed to rest. Children should not be allowed to interfere with the pup when he is

These two Whippet babies look very content resting in the arms of their beloved owner.

Keeping your curious puppy in a confined area will prevent trouble, but make sure that it is large enough for him to move around comfortably and play.

sleeping. If the pup is not tired, he can be allowed to investigate his new home—but always under your close supervision. After a short look around, the puppy will no doubt appreciate a light meal and a drink of water. Do not overfeed him at his first meal because he will be in an excited state and more likely to be sick.

Although it is an obvious temptation, you should not invite friends and neighbors around to see the new arrival until he has had at least 48 hours in which to settle down. Indeed, if you can delay this longer then do so, especially if the puppy is not fully vaccinated. At the very least, the visitors might introduce some local bacteria on their clothing that the puppy is not immune to. This aspect is always a risk when a pup has been moved some distance, so the fewer people the pup meets in the first week or so the better.

DANGERS IN THE HOME

Your home holds many potential dangers for a little mischievous puppy, so you must think about these in advance and be sure he is protected from them. The more obvious are as follows:

Open Fires. All open fires should be protected by a mesh screen guard so there is no danger of the pup being burned by spitting pieces of coal or wood.

Electrical Wires. Puppies just love chewing on things, so be sure that all electrical appliances are neatly hidden from view and are not left plugged in when not in use. It is not sufficient simply to turn the plug switch to the off position—pull the plug from the socket.

Open Doors. A door would seem a pretty innocuous object, yet with a strong draft it could kill or injure a puppy easily if it is slammed shut. Always ensure there is no risk of this happening. It is most likely during warm weather when you have windows or outside doors open and a sudden gust of wind blows through.

Balconies. If you live in a high-rise building, obviously the pup must be protected from falling. Be sure he cannot get through any railings on your patio, balcony, or deck.

Ponds and Pools. A garden pond or a swimming pool is a very dangerous place for a little puppy to be near. Be sure it is well screened so there is no risk of the pup falling in. It takes barely a minute for a pup—or a child—to drown.

The Kitchen. While many puppies will be kept in the kitchen, at least while they are toddlers and not able

Opposite: Because of their gentle nature, Whippets make excellent pets and can be trusted around your child. This happy family gets ready for a walk outside.

Although children and puppies adore one another, it's vital that you teach your child early the proper way to handle a delicate puppy.

to control their bowel movements, this is a room full of danger—especially while you are cooking. When cooking, keep the puppy in a play pen or in another room where he is safely out of harm's way. Alternatively, if you have a carry box or crate, put him in this so he can still see you but is well protected.

Be aware, when using washing machines, that more than one puppy has clambered in and decided to have a nap and received a wash instead! If you leave the washing machine door open and leave the room for any reason, then be sure to check inside the machine before you close the door and switch on.

Small Children. Toddlers and small children should never be left unsupervised with puppies. In spite of such advice it is amazing just how many people not only do this but also allow children to pull and maul pups. They should be taught from the outset that a puppy is not a plaything to be dragged about the home—and they should be promptly scolded if they disobey.

Children must be shown how to lift a puppy so it is safe. Failure by you to correctly educate your children about dogs could one day result in their getting a very nasty bite or scratch. When a puppy is lifted, his weight must always be supported. To lift the pup, first

There's nothing more adorable than a basket full of Whippet puppies. Because of their fragility in the early stages, puppies need a lot of tender loving care and special guidance.

place your right hand under his chest. Next, secure the pup by using your left hand to hold his neck. Now you can lift him and bring him close to your chest. Never lift a pup by his ears and, while he can be lifted by the scruff of his neck where the fur is loose, there is no reason ever to do this, so don't.

Beyond the dangers already cited you may be able to think of other ones that are specific to your home— steep basement steps or the like. Go around your home and check out all potential problems—you'll be glad you did.

THE FIRST NIGHT

The first few nights a puppy spends away from his mother and littermates are quite traumatic for him. He will feel very lonely, maybe cold, and will certainly miss the heartbeat of his siblings when sleeping. To help overcome his loneliness it may help to place a clock next to his bed—one with a loud tick. This will in some way soothe him, as the clock ticks to a rhythm not dissimilar from a heart beat. A cuddly toy may also help in the first few weeks. A dim nightlight may

Two Whippets are better than one—at least in this case. If you do have another pet at home, it's best to introduce him to your new puppy under careful supervision. They'll soon become fast friends!

provide some comfort to the puppy, because his eyes will not yet be fully able to see in the dark. The puppy may want to leave his bed for a drink or to relieve himself.

The way a puppy acts with his littermates or other dogs can tell you a lot about his personality.

If the pup does whimper in the night, there are two things you should not do. One is to get up and chastise him, because he will not understand why you are shouting at him; and the other is to rush to comfort him every time he cries because he will quickly realize that if he wants you to come running all he needs to do is to holler loud enough!

By all means give your puppy some extra attention on his first night, but after this quickly refrain from so doing. The pup will cry for a while but then settle down and go to sleep. Some pups are, of course, worse than others in this respect, so you must use balanced judgment in the matter. Many owners take their pups to bed with them, and there is certainly nothing wrong with this.

The pup will be no trouble in such cases. However, you should only do this if you intend to let this be a permanent arrangement, otherwise it is hardly fair to the puppy. If you have decided to have two puppies, then they will keep each other company and you will have few problems.

OTHER PETS

If you have other pets in the home then the puppy must be introduced to them under careful supervision. Puppies will get on just fine with any other pets— but you must make due allowance for the respective sizes of the pets concerned, and appreciate that your puppy has a rather playful nature. It would be very foolish to leave him with a young rabbit. The pup will want to play and might bite the bunny and get altogether too rough with it. Kittens are more able to defend themselves from overly cheeky pups, who will get a quick scratch if they overstep the mark. The adult cat could obviously give the pup a very bad scratch, though generally cats will jump clear of pups and watch them from a suitable vantage point. Eventually they will meet at ground level where the cat will quickly hiss and box a puppy's ears. The pup will soon learn to respect an adult cat; thereafter they will probably develop into great friends as the pup matures into an adult dog.

Housetraining a puppy is no easy task, however, with time and patience, it can be completed successfully.

HOUSETRAINING

Undoubtedly, the first form of training your puppy will undergo is in respect to his toilet habits. To achieve this you can use either newspaper, or a large litter tray filled with soil or lined with newspaper. A puppy cannot control his bowels until he is a few months old, and not fully until he is an adult. Therefore you must anticipate his needs and be prepared for a few accidents. The prime times a pup will urinate and defecate are shortly after he wakes up from a sleep, shortly after he has eaten, and after he has been playing awhile. He will usually whimper and start searching the room for a suitable place. You must quickly pick him up and place him on the newspaper or in the litter tray. Hold him in position gently but firmly. He might jump out of the box without doing anything on the first one or two occasions, but if you simply repeat the procedure every time you think he wants to relieve himself then eventually he will get the message.

When he does defecate as required, give him plenty of praise, telling him what a good puppy he

This little puppy is lucky to have both his mother and caring owner beside him every step of the way.

Losing your dog is something that no family wants to experience, so take special precautions to keep your dog properly identified and safely confined when off lead.

is. The litter tray or newspaper must, of course, be cleaned or replaced after each use—puppies do not like using a dirty toilet any more than you do. The pup's toilet can be placed near the kitchen door and as he gets older the tray can be placed outside while the door is open. The pup will then start to use it while he is outside. From that time on, it is easy to get the pup to use a given area of the yard.

Many breeders recommend the popular alternative of crate training. Upon bringing the pup home, introduce him to his crate. The open wire crate is the best choice, placed in a restricted, draft-free area of the home. Put the pup's Nylabone® and other favorite toys in the crate along with a wool blanket or other suitable bedding. The puppy's natural cleanliness instincts prohibit him from soiling in the place where he sleeps, his crate. The puppy should be allowed to go in and out of the open crate during the day, but he should sleep in the crate at the night and at other intervals during the day.

Whenever the pup is taken out of his crate, he should be brought outside (or to his newspapers) to do his business. Never use the crate as a place of punishment. You will see how quickly your pup takes to his crate, considering it as his own safe haven from the big world around him.

THE EARLY DAYS

You will no doubt be given much advice on how to bring up your puppy. This will come from dog-owning friends, neighbors, and through articles and books you may read on the subject. Some of the advice will be sound, some will be nothing short of rubbish. What you should do above all else is to keep an open mind and let common sense prevail over prejudice and worn-out ideas that have been handed down over the centuries. There is no one way that is superior to all others, no more than there is no one dog that is exactly a replica of another. Each is an individual and must always be regarded as such.

A dog never becomes disobedient, unruly, or a menace to society without the full consent of his owner. Your puppy may have many limitations, but the singular biggest limitation he is confronted with in so many instances is his owner's inability to understand his needs and how to cope with them.

IDENTIFICATION

It is a sad reflection on our society that the number of dogs and cats stolen every year runs into many thousands. To these can be added the number that get lost. If you do not want your cherished pet to be lost or stolen, then you should see that he is carrying a permanent identification number, as well as a temporary tag on his collar.

Permanent markings come in the form of tattoos placed either inside the pup's ear flap, or on the inner side of a pup's upper rear leg. The number given is then recorded with one of the national registration companies. Research laboratories will not purchase dogs carrying numbers as they realize these are clearly someone's pet, and not abandoned animals. As a result, thieves will normally abandon dogs so marked and this at least gives the dog a chance to be taken to the police or the dog pound, when the number can be traced and the dog reunited with its family. The only problem with this method at this time is that there are a number of registration bodies, so it is not always apparent which one the dog is registered with (as you provide the actual number). However, each registration body is aware of his competitors and will normally be happy to supply their addresses. Those holding the dog can check out which one you are with. It is not a perfect system, but until such is developed it's the best available.

Another permanent form of identification is the microchip, a computer chip that is no bigger than a grain of rice that is injected between the dog's shoulder blades. The dog feels no discomfort. The dog also receives a tag that says he is microchipped. If the dog is lost and picked up by the humane society, they can trace the owner by scanning the microchip. It is the safest form of identification.

A temporary tag takes the form of a metal or plastic disk large enough for you to place the dog's name and your phone number on it—maybe even your address as well. In virtually all places you will be required to obtain a license for your puppy. This may not become applicable until the pup is six months old, but it might apply regardless of his age. Much depends upon the state within a country, or the country itself, so check with your veterinarian if the breeder has not already advised you on this.

The newest method of identification is the microchip, a computer chip that is no bigger than a grain of rice, that is injected into the dog's skin.

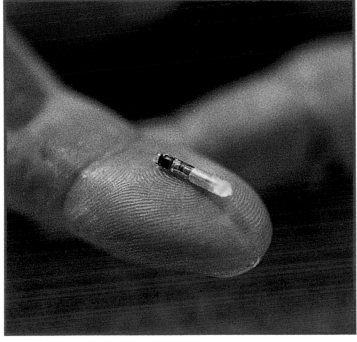

CARING FOR YOUR WHIPPET

FEEDING THE PUPPY AND ADULT WHIPPET

I cannot emphasize enough how important it is to feed you new Whippet properly. In order for your puppy to develop both physically and mentally and reach his full potential, a nutritional diet is necessary. Upon your new puppy's arrival, he will soon need to eat. Remember to check with the breeder or previous owner of the dog as to what type of food the dog is used to eating and how much. If you choose to deviate from the dog's original diet, make sure the change is gradual. Slowly mixing a few tablespoons of the new

Good nutrition is vital for a puppy's growth. Knowing the correct amount of food to feed your Whippet puppy and the necessary vitamins and nutrients that should be included in his diet is important for a healthy beginning.

food with the old food every day will help make the transition easier. A Whippet puppy will thrive on almost any good brand of commercial dog food. A combination of vitamins and other supplements added to the food is strongly encouraged.

Following the breeder's feeding instructions is extremely important. As the puppy gets older, the number of meals he eats should slowly decrease. In the beginning, newborn puppies will need to be fed small quantities of food at frequent intervals. A chubby Whippet puppy is a good indication that you're feeding him properly; you don't want a thin puppy. Whippet puppies grow so quickly and burn off tremendous amounts of energy, so a little extra weight will do them good. On the other hand, the adult Whippet's eating habits will decrease as growth slows.

Some dog owners believe that table scraps are a wonderful alternative to commercialized dog food, but like anything else, table scraps given in excess often spell trouble, creating a spoiled dog that may become obese and ill. Believe me, there's nothing more disturbing than an obese Whippet. Most local pet stores, veterinary offices, and dog shows sell some of the best-commercialized dog foods available. Most of these foods are nutritionally complete, allowing a balanced diet for dogs of all ages without any extras needed. Naturally, a hard biscuit or milkbone everyday as a treat is acceptable and encouraged.

POPpups™ are 100 percent edible and enhanced with dog-friendly ingredients like liver, cheese, spinach, chicken, carrots, or potatoes. They contain NO salt, sugar, alcohol, plastic or preservatives. You can even microwave a POPpup™ to turn into a huge crackly treat.

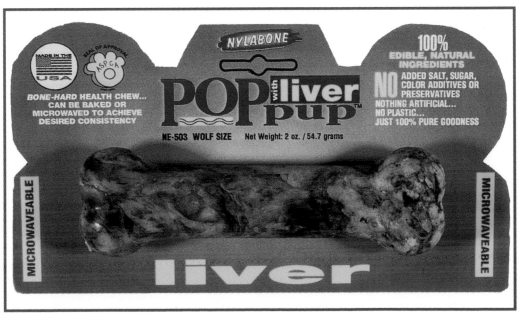

All dogs look forward to mealtime. Make feeding a positive experience by providing your dog with nutritious food, clean bowls, and fresh water.

How Much to Feed and When

The amount of feeding intervals will decrease as the Whippet matures. One main meal consisting of two to two and one-half cups of dry food mixed with a little warm water (for moisture) and canned food is sufficient for any adult Whippet. Depending on the dog's weight, amounts may vary from dog to dog and you'll get a feel for whether you need to cut down or increase feedings. If the top two or three spine bones are not visible on your adult Whippet's back, you're probably overfeeding him. This is a good guideline in determining your dog's correct weight. A perfectly conditioned Whippet should be muscular with just enough weight to present a smooth flowing outline. The time of the adult's main meal is not that important—late afternoon or early evening has always worked best for me. Just remember that if you feed

Carrots are rich in fiber, carbohydrates, and vitamin A. The Carrot Bone™ by Nylabone® is a durable chew containing no plastics or artificial ingredients and it can be served as-is, in a bone-hard form, or microwaved to a biscuit consistency.

your Whippet at a certain time everyday, you should try to be consistent, deviating as little as possible from the time of your feedings. Some Whippet owners that work during the day provide their dog with a small bowl of dry food. This way, the dogs can serve themselves when they're feeling hungry. It's important not to leave out any canned food for a long period because it will spoil.

Table Scraps: Pros and Cons

As I mentioned earlier, excessive amounts of table scraps can be very harmful to your Whippet. Foods

The time of day you choose to feed your Whippet is not important, provided you maintain a consistent schedule.

that are bad for us are usually also bad for our dogs. Junk food such as candy, chocolate, potato chips, and other snack foods should always be avoided. Any spicy, fried, or starchy foods should also be avoided. Extra vegetables, chicken, or beef are nutritional table scraps that may be offered if you need to do so. Do keep in mind that the best alternative is to stick to the commercial dog foods and provide minimal people scraps. If you have any questions regarding what type of commercial foods to purchase, contact the breeder of the dog or your local veterinarian.

An expecting mother needs a diet high in protein and vitamins to keep herself and her puppies healthy.

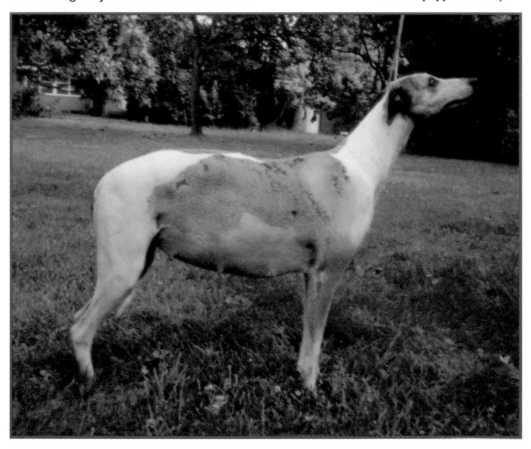

How to Feed

Believe it or not, there are proper feeding techniques and some helpful hints that may make things easier, especially if you're feeding more than one dog. If you're a Whippet owner, that's usually the case because one Whippet is just not enough! Like people, dogs can be bullies and slobs when it comes to chow time. A pack of Whippets can get worked up to the point of semi-aggressiveness during feeding time and precautions should be taken for all the animals' safety.

This pretty puppy is looking for some leftover Halloween candy but food that is bad for a human is bad for your dog. Although giving your Whippet table scraps occasionally is acceptable, do not make it a habit.

If you have more than one dog, it's best to separate the dogs during feeding, giving them their own private eating space. This will help avoid any fighting between the dogs and one dog getting far more to eat than the other. Another feeding tip that may prove helpful is refrigerating uneaten portions of canned food to prevent spoilage. Discard any uneaten food out of your dog's bowl after he's eaten and make sure to wash the dog's bowl thoroughly with soap and water. It is also important to remember to provide clean, fresh water at all times. Frequently, new puppies or dogs that have just been purchased will take some time adjusting to the water if they're not from the area. Dog food may be presented to your Whippet in many different bowl shapes and sizes. Just remem-

ber that there must be enough room for the dog to fit his head comfortably inside the bowl. Weighted stainless steel bowls often fit neatly into holders and prevent your new Whippet from dumping his dinner in an inappropriate spot.

These Whippets' good behavior and training is evident as they patiently wait their turn to show off.

ACCOMMODATIONS FOR THE WHIPPET

Inside or Out?

Although the Whippet has such short hair, they can easily acclimate to cooler temperatures. Even on cold winter days, I allow my dogs a little time to play outside. Small Whippet puppies that are newly weaned from their mother may be placed outside during the warmer months, but kept inside in colder temperatures because they are likely to catch a chill quicker than the adults. During the night, the Whippet should have a warm sheltered area to retreat to. If you choose not to bring the dog inside, an outside kennel or basement is sufficient as long as the dog or dogs have a comfortable bed or blanket to sleep on. Whippets like to sleep in a group and will often pile on top of each other for maximum warmth and comfort. Although you might not like it, the most desired accommodation for your Whippet is your own personal bed. Whippets love to sleep not only in the bed, but also under the sheets. It's amazing that even on the warmest summer nights, a Whippet will insist on digging under the covers to sleep by your side.

The Crate

The most useful piece of canine equipment is the dog crate. Most crates are made of wire or plastic, are available in many different sizes, and are easily collapsible for transporting. The crate is very efficient for housing both the puppy and adult Whippet. Not only does it offer a safe place for your dog to stay when left unattended, but it is also a good place for the dog to eat and sleep. Unfortunately, many pet owners feel guilty for placing their new dogs in such a confined area. If you choose not to use a crate and allow the pup to roam around the house unsupervised, you may be creating your own disaster. One day of your new dog chewing the sofa, bedroom rugs, and the TV remote control should be enough to convince you that puppies need to be crated.

Because of their short coats, Whippets can be affected by cooler temperatures. A jacket can help keep your Whippet warm on those cold and blustery days.

It isn't difficult to get your puppy or adult dog acquainted with his crate. Place the crate in a convenient location with the door open. Cover the bottom of the crate with comfortable bedding and perhaps some of the dog's favorite toys. Allow the dog to investigate the crate, locking him in periodically for short intervals. Also, try feeding the dog while he is inside the crate. In only a short frame of time, the dog will adjust to the crate, often seeking it out for safety and peace of mind. Keep in mind that if you intend to leave the dog crated for several hours, you should provide him with some water. Dogs that are placed in crates at an early age learn to accept it as part of their lives and actually enjoy the privacy.

Unlike some breeds, Whippets prefer to sleep within groups and can often be found cuddled together for comfort and security.

Indoor/Outdoor Kennel Runs

Another popular living arrangement for the Whippet is an indoor/outdoor kennel run. This fenced-in yard space attached to your house by a swinging pet door allows the Whippet the comfort and access of both indoor and outdoor accommodations. Such a facility enables the dog to enjoy the benefits of fresh air and exercise during the day and warmth and shelter during the night. A doghouse or crate may also be placed inside the kennel run for extra comfort. This type of kennel facility also allows the dog easy access to the bathroom while you're at work or out for the day.

Cleanliness

On of the most important factors in having adequate accommodations for the Whippet is cleanliness. By nature, the Whippet is a very clean dog. It's repulsive when a dog is kept in unsanitary conditions. Whether it be a kennel run, doghouse, or dog bed, the immediate surroundings must be kept as clean as possible at all times. This involves daily removal of any dog excrement, frequent changing of bedding, and scrubbing and washing of dog bowls and kennel floors. A clean dog environment will help ward off pesty critters such as flies, fleas, ticks, and mice.

Using a crate can be very effective when trying to housetrain your Whippet. You can make the crate more cozy and inviting by placing some blankets and your dog's favorite toys inside of it.

EXERCISE

The Whippet needs adequate space to exercise on a daily basis and depriving him of a daily run or brisk walk is unhealthy and unnatural. Although a large fenced-in yard or field is ideal for exercising, the Whippet does not need a vast space. Those who do not have the luxury of a large yard can still properly exercise their dogs. A 20- to 30-minute walk every day or every other day will be adequate exercise and will make your Whippet a lot happier and easier to live with. You will learn how to tell when the dog needs to get out and stretch his legs for a quick sprint. Bringing a Frisbee™ or a ball along can add a lot of diversity to your dog's exercise routine. Because of their agility, Whippets are adept at playing Frisbee™. It does not take much time at all to teach the Whippet to run and retrieve a ball or Frisbee™ and quickly return it to you, anxiously awaiting another toss. For people that enjoy jogging, the Whippet is a superior running companion when conditioned properly, capable of running great distances with relative ease. Another method, which I have often used in conditioning my Whippets, is roadworking. I believe that there is no better exercise that gets your dog into tiptop shape in such a short period. Roadworking can be done using either a bicycle or the back of a truck. In both instances, the dog is attached to a leash and is allowed to follow behind the bike or truck as you drive along at

A wetdown coat will help keep your Whippet cool in warm temperatures.

Opposite: Exercise not only improves a dog's physical appearance; it also helps to relieve stress and boredom. Setting aside time for your Whippet to exercise is extremely beneficial to the quality of his life.

a very slow speed. Roadworking involves a bit of practice and skill before both you and the dog can exercise safely and confidently, but the results are astonishing. Your Whippet will gain amazing muscle tone and soundness. It's also useful in preparing a dog for the show ring.

The Nylabone® Frisbee™ is a must-have if you want to have fun with your dog.

Special exercise time is essential for dogs that are housebound most of the day while their owners are at work. Not only is exercise important for an animal's physical weight, but it also helps to relieve stress and tension he may have been building up while you were away. Setting aside time everyday to play with the dog will also give him something to look forward to. Like people, dogs can become depressed and bored and need play and exercise time to keep them happy. Just remember that the dog should never be overworked during hot days and exercise during these periods should be kept to a minimum.

As a Whippet owner, you should make sure that your dog receives the proper amount of exercise on a daily basis. There are many fun activities, such as playing Frisbee™, which you and your Whippet can do as a team.

GROOMING THE WHIPPET

Grooming is an essential part of any dog's care. Fortunately for their owners, because of their short coats Whippets require very little grooming time.

The Whippet is one of the easiest breeds of dog to groom. Its short coat allows for none of the hassles associated with long-haired breeds, such as mats and excessive shedding. Your Whippet will shed very little as long as his coat is kept in good condition. This can be achieved by keeping your dog on a healthy, nutritious diet and bathing him on a bi-weekly basis.

Whether you're preparing your dog for the show ring or just giving him his weekly touch-up, you should start by brushing the dog with a rubber or soft brush or a "hound glove." If a brush or glove is not available, a gentle rubdown with your fingers will do the trick in removing loose dead skin and hair. Not only do the dogs love the rubdown, but their coats shine as well. While you brush the Whippet you may want to consider doing a flea and tick check.

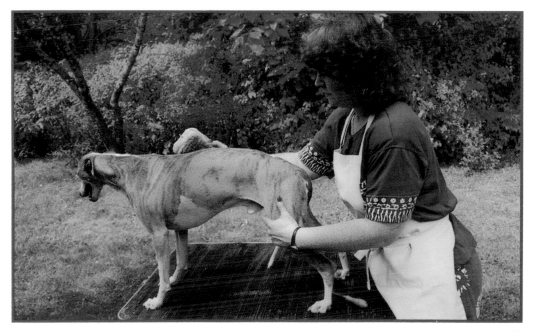

FLEA AND TICK CONTROL

Dogs that are kept in wooded and grassy areas will often pick up wood ticks or fleas. Fortunately, the Whippet's short hair makes the hunt for these parasites a lot easier. Don't panic if you do find some ticks and fleas, but a complete flea and tick treatment will be needed. You may begin by treating the outside yard with a flea and tick spray available at your local pet store. The next step will be to spray the inside of your home or kennel and anywhere the dog spends a great deal of time. The final step will be to treat the dog with flea and tick insecticides, but you must be extremely careful in selecting such products. Like the Greyhound, the Whippet's narrow chest cavity can make them vulnerable to illness or even death if the chemicals are too strong. Make sure to contact your veterinarian for his suggestion as to what products to use and how much. There are several all-natural flea and tick products available that are strongly recommended for the Whippet breed.

Opposite: Although nail clipping can be the Whippet's least favorite part of grooming, you can make the experience more bearable by beginning the process at a very early age.

When grooming your Whippet, make sure to look for any fleas and ticks. The Whippet's short coat helps to make this inspection much easier.

BATHING & NAIL CLIPPING

Bathing an eight-week-old Whippet puppy, or some adults for that matter, can be one of the most challenging feats for a Whippet owner. Some Whippets love to get a bath while others simply hate it. It won't take long to find out if your dog will tolerate the bathing experience. I've seen Whippets do everything from lunging several feet in the air to purposely kicking out all four legs in hope of escaping the bathtub. A noose placed securely, but not too tightly, around the animal's neck, attached to a metal bolt is necessary. This will keep the dog safely in place without the risk of him jumping out and injuring himself. It's best to start bathing the Whippets when they're puppies to get them used to it. Hopefully, at this young age, they can learn how to behave while they're being washed. Bathing water should be lukewarm and gently poured over the animal, intending not to upset him. A special dog shampoo then may be applied to the dog. Depending on the purpose of the bath, a scented, medicated, or flea and tick shampoo may be used. For the best results, be sure to let the lathered-up dog sit for six to ten minutes before rinsing him.

You will need to cut your Whippet's nails at least once every two weeks to prevent tearing and possible damage to your dog's paws.

If there's one other part of the grooming process that the Whippet may hate more than the bathtub, it's nail clipping. Again, the key to having your dog stand still during this important grooming procedure is to start him at an early age. Nail cutting at least once every two weeks is very important. Begin by placing the puppy on a sturdy grooming table, encouraging him to stand. Place the Whippet under one arm while holding each foot securely and clip away. Clip as close to the quick as you can. The quick is the dark vein that runs inside the dog's nail and is visible to the eye. If you cut the nail too close and it begins to bleed, you can apply some quick stop powder or cornstarch to stop the bleeding. The Whippet's nails will grow extremely long very quickly if not cut on a regular basis. Long nails not only look unattractive but can also damage the Whippet's paw. Other methods of shortening nails include using a filer or an electric nail grinder, which should only be used by an experienced

The model example of how a dog should behave on the grooming table, this Whippet stands patiently while his whiskers are trimmed. This procedure enhances the smooth outline of the head.

individual. Although it's not necessary, trimming the Whippet's whiskers and facial hair will enhance the smooth outline of the head. Frequently, show exhibitors can be seen trimming away at dog shows. A small pair of blunt scissors will do the trick and won't cut the dog severely if he were to suddenly jerk away. Some Whippet owners even choose to trim other areas of the dog such as the tail, neck, and ears for a cleaner look. Brushing the teeth is also an important part of Whippet grooming. A small toothbrush dipped in peroxide or commercialized dog toothpaste can be applied to the dog's teeth. Brushing on a weekly basis helps remove tartar buildup on the teeth and gums.

Only a previous owner of perhaps a Shetland Sheepdog or Collie will truly appreciate the ease of grooming the Whippet in comparison to other breeds. Besides a simple bath, nail clipping, and a quick brush, grooming a Whippet requires very little work.

Opposite: Taking care of your Whippet is a serious commitment. It's up to you, as his owner, to attend to all of his grooming needs.

Brushing your Whippet's teeth not only prevents bad breath, but helps to eliminate tartar and plaque build-up.

TRAINING YOUR WHIPPET

Once your puppy has settled into your home and responds to his name, then you can begin his basic training. Before giving advice on how you should go about doing this, two important points should be made. You should train the puppy in isolation of any potential distractions, and you should keep all lessons very short. It is essential that you have the full attention of your puppy. This is not possible if there

Every pet owner desires a well-behaved, obedient dog. For the best results, begin training your new Whippet as soon as possible.

Training your Whippet to a leash and collar allows you more control when walking him. Once he is leash trained, you can move on to basic obedience.

are other people about, or televisions and radios on, or other pets in the vicinity. Even when the pup has become a young adult, the maximum time you should allocate to a lesson is about 20 minutes. However, you can give the puppy more than one lesson a day, three being as many as are recommended, each well spaced apart.

Before beginning a lesson, always play a little game with the puppy so he is in an active state of mind and thus more receptive to the matter at hand. Likewise, always end a lesson with fun-time for the pup, and always—this is most important—end on a high note, praising the puppy. Let the lesson end when the pup has done as you require so he receives lots of fuss. This will really build his confidence.

COLLAR AND LEASH TRAINING

Training a puppy to his collar and leash is very easy. Place a collar on the puppy and, although he will initially try to bite at it, he will soon forget it, the more so if you play with him. You can leave the collar on for a few hours. Some people leave their dogs' collars on all of the time, others only when they are taking the dog out. If it is to be left on, purchase a narrow or round one so it does not mark the fur.

Having your Whippet leash and collar trained is good for you and your dog, both for his safety and the safety of others.

Once the puppy ignores his collar, then you can attach the leash to it and let the puppy pull this along behind it for a few minutes. However, if the pup starts to chew at the leash, simply hold the leash but keep it slack and let the pup go where he wants. The idea is to let him get the feel of the leash, but not get in the habit of chewing it. Repeat this a couple of times a day for two days and the pup will get used to the leash without thinking that it will restrain him—which you will not have attempted to do yet.

Next, you can let the pup understand that the leash will restrict his movements. The first time he realizes this, he will pull and buck or just sit down. Immediately call the pup to you and give him lots of fuss. Never tug on the leash so the puppy is dragged along the floor, as this simply implants a negative thought in his mind.

THE COME COMMAND

Come is the most vital of all commands and especially so for the independently minded dog. To teach the puppy to come, let him reach the end of a long lead, then give the command and his name, gently pulling him toward you at the same time. As soon as he associates the word come with the action of moving toward you, pull only when he does not respond immediately. As he starts to come, move back to make him learn that he must come from a distance as well as when he is close to you. Soon you may be able to practice without a leash, but if he is slow to come or notably disobedient, go to him and pull him toward you, repeating the command. Never scold a dog during this exercise—or any other exercise. Remember the trick is that the puppy must want to come to you. For the very independent dog, hand signals may work better than verbal commands.

A training class is not only a great way to start basic obedience, it is also the perfect place to socialize your Whippet with other dogs.

THE SIT COMMAND

As with most basic commands, your puppy will learn this one in just a few lessons. You can give the puppy two lessons a day on the sit command but he will make just as much progress with one 15-minute lesson each day. Some trainers will advise you that you should not proceed to other commands until the previous one has been learned really well. However, a bright young pup is quite capable of handling more than one command per lesson, and certainly per day. Indeed, as time progresses, you will be going through each command as a matter of routine before a new one is attempted. This is so the puppy always starts, as well as ends, a lesson on a high note, having successfully completed something.

Opposite: When it comes to training your Whippet, remember to always be patient, maintain consistency, and to praise the puppy for a job well done.

This Whippet demonstrates the sit command with ease. Your puppy should be able to learn this basic command in only a few lessons.

Call the puppy to you and fuss over him. Place one hand on his hindquarters and the other under his upper chest. Say "Sit" in a pleasant (never harsh) voice. At the same time, push down his rear end and push up under his chest. Now lavish praise on the puppy. Repeat this a few times and your pet will get the idea. Once the puppy is in the sit position you will release your hands. At first he will tend to get up, so immediately repeat the exercise. The lesson will end when the pup is in the sit position. When the puppy understands the command, and does it right away, you can slowly move backwards so that you are a few feet away from him. If he attempts to come to you, simply place him back in the original position and start again. Do not attempt to keep the pup in the sit position for too long. At this age, even a few seconds is a long while and you do not want him to get bored with lessons before he has even begun them.

A well-trained dog will be able to walk on a leash without pulling and tugging you along. Teaching your Whippet the heel command make your daily walks a pleasant experience.

THE HEEL COMMAND

All dogs should be able to walk nicely on a leash without their owners being involved in a tug-of-war. The heel command will follow leash training. Heel training is best done where you have a wall to one side of you. This will restrict the puppy's lateral movements, so you only have to contend with forward and backward situations. A fence is an alternative, or you can do the lesson in the garage. Again, it is better to do the lesson in private, not on a public sidewalk where there will be many distractions.

Opposite: The Whippet's intelligence and eagerness to please makes him an ideal candidate for basic training.

With a puppy, there will be no need to use a choke collar as you can be just as effective with a regular one. The leash should be of good length, certainly not too short. You can adjust the space between you, the puppy, and the wall so your pet has only a small amount of room to move sideways. This being so, he will either hang back or pull ahead—the latter is the more desirable state as it indicates a bold pup who is not frightened of you.

Hold the leash in your right hand and pass it through your left. As the puppy moves ahead and strains on the leash, give the leash a quick jerk backwards with your left hand, at the same time saying "Heel." The position you want the pup to be in is such that his chest is level with, or just behind, an imaginary line from your knee. When the puppy is in this position, praise him and begin walking again, and the whole exercise will be repeated. Once the puppy begins to get the message, you can use your left hand to pat the side of your knee so the pup is encouraged to keep close to your side.

It is useful to suddenly do an about-turn when the pup understands the basics. The puppy will now be behind you, so you can pat your knee and say "Heel." As soon as the pup is in the correct position, give him lots of praise. The puppy will now be beginning to associate certain words with certain actions. Whenever he is not in the heel position he will experience displeasure as you jerk the leash, but when he comes alongside you he will receive praise. Given these two options, he will always prefer the latter—assuming he has no other reason to fear you, which would then create a dilemma in his mind.

Once the lesson has been well learned, then you can adjust your pace from a slow walk to a quick one and the puppy will come to adjust. The slow walk is always the more difficult for most puppies, as they are usually anxious to be on the move.

If you have no wall to walk against then things will be a little more difficult because the pup will tend to wander to his left. This means you need to give lateral jerks as well as bring the pup to your side. End the lesson when the pup is walking nicely beside you. Begin the lesson with a few sit commands (which he understands by now), so you're starting with success and praise. If your puppy is nervous on the leash, you should never drag him to your side as you may see so many other people do (who obviously didn't invest in a good book like you did!). If the pup sits down, call him to your side and give lots of praise. The pup must always come to you because he wants to. If he is dragged to your side he will see you doing the dragging—a big negative. When he races ahead he does not see you jerk the leash, so all he knows is that something restricted his movement and, once he was in a given position, you gave him lots of praise. This is using canine psychology to your advantage.

Always try to remember that if a dog must be disciplined, then try not to let him associate the discipline with you. This is not possible in all matters but, where it is, this is definitely to be preferred.

Taking the time to teach your Whippet the basic commands properly will be beneficial in all aspects of your life together. A well-mannered dog will be welcomed anywhere—especially the show ring.

THE STAY COMMAND

This command follows from the sit. Face the puppy and say "Sit." Now step backwards, and as you do, say "Stay." Let the pup remain in the position for only a few seconds before calling him to you and giving lots of praise. Repeat this, but step further back. You do not need to shout at the puppy. Your pet is not deaf; in fact, his hearing is far better than yours. Speak just loudly enough for the pup to hear, yet use a firm voice. You can stretch the word to form a "sta-a-a-y." If the pup gets up and comes to you simply lift him up, place him back in the original position, and start again. As the pup comes to understand the command, you can move further and further back.

Obedience is absolutely necessary when your dog is in the show ring. These handlers help their Whippets get ready to display their talents.

The next test is to walk away after placing the pup. This will mean your back is to him, which will tempt him to follow you. Keep an eye over your shoulder, and the minute the pup starts to move, spin around and, using a sterner voice, say either "Sit" or "Stay." If the pup has gotten quite close to you, then, again, return him to the original position.

At first, your puppy doesn't have to remain in the "stay" position for more than two or three minutes. As time goes by, you can gradually increase the time that he stays.

As the weeks go by you can increase the length of time the pup is left in the stay position—but two to three minutes is quite long enough for a puppy. If your puppy drops into a lying position and is clearly more comfortable, there is nothing wrong with this. Likewise, your pup will want to face the direction in which you walked off. Some trainers will insist that the dog faces the direction he was placed in, regardless of whether you move off on his blind side. I have never believed in this sort of obedience because it has no practical benefit.

THE DOWN COMMAND

From the puppy's viewpoint, the down command can be one of the more difficult ones to accept. This is because the position is one taken up by a submissive dog in a wild pack situation. A timid dog will roll over—a natural gesture of submission. A bolder pup will want to get up, and might back off, not feeling he should have to submit to this command. He will feel that he is under attack from you and about to be

punished—which is what would be the position in his natural environment. Once he comes to understand this is not the case, he will accept this unnatural position without any problem.

You may notice that some dogs will sit very quickly, but will respond to the down command more slowly— it is their way of saying that they will obey the command, but under protest!

There two ways to teach this command. One is, in my mind, more intimidating than the other, but it is up to you to decide which one works best for you. The first method is to stand in front of your puppy and bring him to the sit position, with his collar and leash on. Pass the leash under your left foot so that when you pull on it, the result is that the pup's neck is forced downwards. With your free left hand, push the pup's shoulders down while at the same time saying "Down." This is when a bold pup will instantly try to back off and wriggle in full protest. Hold the pup firmly by the shoulders so he stays in the position for a second or two, then tell him what a good dog he is and give him

Accepting the down position can be very difficult for a dog because he has to be submissive. This handsome duo has no problem staying "down" for the camera.

The consummate show dog, the Whippet is the picture of charm and dignity.

lots of praise. Repeat this only a few times in a lesson because otherwise the puppy will get bored and upset over this command. End with an easy command that brings back the pup's confidence.

The second method, and the one I prefer, is done as follows: Stand in front of the pup and then tell him to sit. Now kneel down, which is immediately far less intimidating to the puppy than to have you towering above him. Take each of his front legs and pull them forward, at the same time saying "Down." Release the legs and quickly apply light pressure on the shoulders with your left hand. Then, as quickly, say "Good boy" and give lots of fuss. Repeat two or three times only. The pup will learn over a few lessons. Remember, this is a very submissive act on the pup's behalf, so there is no need to rush matters.

RECALL TO HEEL COMMAND

When your puppy is coming to the heel position from an off-leash situation—such as if he has been running free—he should do this in the correct manner. He should pass behind you and take up his position and then sit. To teach this command, have the pup in front of you in the sit position with his collar and leash on. Hold the leash in your right hand. Give him the command to heel, and pat your left knee. As the pup starts to move forward, use your right hand to guide him behind you. If need be you can hold his collar and walk the dog around the back of you to the desired position. You will need to repeat this a few times until the dog understands what is wanted.

When he has done this a number of times, you can try it without the collar and leash. If the pup comes up toward your left side, then bring him to the sit position in front of you, hold his collar and walk him around the

Agility and speed are two of the Whippet's greatest attributes. Crystal, owned by Meribeth Metavia, makes it over the high bar with ease.

Whippets enjoy playing in the great outdoors, but danger can occur if you are not careful. It's a good idea to keep your dog on a leash or in a fenced-in area if you can't keep a close eye on him at all times.

back of you. He will eventually understand and automatically pass around your back each time. If the dog is already behind you when you recall him, then he should automatically come to your left side, which you will be patting with your hand.

THE NO COMMAND

This is a command that must be obeyed every time without fail. There are no halfway stages, he must be 100-percent reliable. Most delinquent dogs have never been taught this command; included in these are the jumpers, the barkers, and the biters. Were your puppy to approach a poisonous snake or any other potential danger, the no command, coupled with the recall, could save his life. You do not need to give a specific lesson for this command because it will crop up time and again in day-to-day life.

If the puppy is chewing a slipper, you should approach the pup, take hold of the slipper, and say "No" in a stern voice. If he jumps onto the furniture, lift him off and say "No" and place him gently on the floor. You must be consistent in the use of the command and apply it every time he is doing something you do not want him to do.

YOUR HEALTHY WHIPPET

Dogs, like all other animals, are capable of contracting problems and diseases that, in most cases, are easily avoided by sound husbandry—meaning well-bred and well-cared-for animals are less prone to developing diseases and problems than are carelessly bred and neglected animals. Your knowledge of how to avoid problems is far more valuable than all of the books and advice on how to cure them. Respectively, the only person you should listen to about treatment is your vet. Veterinarians don't have all the answers, but at least they are trained to analyze and treat illnesses, and are aware of the full implications of treatments. This does not mean a few old remedies aren't good standbys when all else fails, but in most cases modern science provides the best treatments for disease.

Opposite: As a responsible Whippet owner, you should have a basic understanding of the medical problems that affect the breed.

PHYSICAL EXAMS

Your puppy should receive regular physical examinations or check-ups. These come in two forms. One is obviously performed by your vet, and the other is a day-to-day procedure that should be done by you. Apart from the fact the exam will highlight any problem at an early stage, it is an excellent way of socializing the pup to being handled.

To do the physical exam yourself, start at the head and work your way around the body. You are looking for any sign of lesions, or any indication of parasites on the pup. The most common parasites are fleas and ticks.

HEALTHY TEETH AND GUMS

Chewing is instinctual. Puppies chew so that their teeth and jaws grow strong and healthy as they develop. As the permanent teeth begin to emerge, it is painful and annoying to the puppy, and puppy owners must recognize that their new charges need something safe upon which to chew. Unfortunately, once the puppy's permanent teeth have emerged and settled solidly into the jaw, the chewing instinct does not fade. Adult dogs instinctively need to clean their teeth, massage their gums, and exercise their jaws through chewing.

It is necessary for your dog to have clean teeth. You should take your dog to the veterinarian at least once a year to have his teeth cleaned and to have his mouth examined for any sign of oral disease. Although dogs do not get cavities in the same way humans do, dogs'

You should examine your Whippet's mouth to make sure that there are no sores, foreign objects, or tooth problems.

The Hercules® by Nylabone® has raised dental tips that help fight plaque on your Whippet's teeth and gums.

teeth accumulate tartar, and more quickly than humans do! Veterinarians recommend brushing your dog's teeth daily. But who can find time to brush their dog's teeth daily? The accumulation of tartar and plaque on our dog's teeth when not removed can cause irritation and eventually erode the enamel and finally destroy the teeth. Advanced cases, while destroying the teeth, bring on gingivitis and periodontitis, two very serious conditions that can affect the dog's internal organs as well...to say nothing about bad breath!

Since everyone can't brush their dog's teeth daily or get to the veterinarian often enough for him to scale

Raised dental tips on the surface of every Plaque Attacker™ help to combat plaque and tartar.

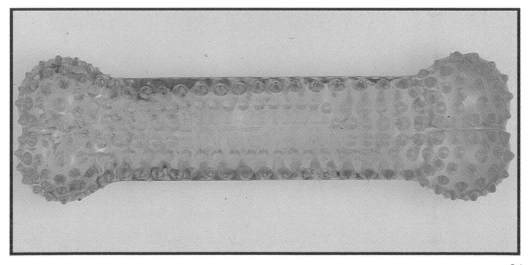

the dog's teeth, providing the dog with something safe to chew on will help maintain oral hygeine. Chew devices from Nylabone® keep dogs' teeth clean, but they also provide an excellent resource for entertainment and relief of doggie tensions. Nylabone® products give your dog something to do for an hour or two every day and during that hour or two, your dog will be taking an active part in keeping his teeth and gums healthy…without even realizing it! That's invaluable to your dog, and valuable to you!

Nylabone® provides fun bones, challenging bones, and *safe* bones. It is an owner's responsibility to recognize safe chew toys from dangerous ones. Your dog will chew and devour anything you give him. Dogs must not be permitted to chew on items that they can break. Pieces of broken objects can do internal damage to a dog, besides ripping the dog's mouth. Cheap plastic or rubber toys can cause stoppage in the intestines; such stoppages are operable only if caught immediately.

The most obvious choices, in this case, may be the worst choice. Natural beef bones were not designed for chewing and cannot take too much pressure from the sides. Due to the abrasive nature of these bones, they should be offered most sparingly. Knuckle bones, though once very popular for dogs, can be easily

Nylabone® is the only plastic dog bone made of 100% virgin nylon, specially processed to create a tough, durable, completely safe bone.

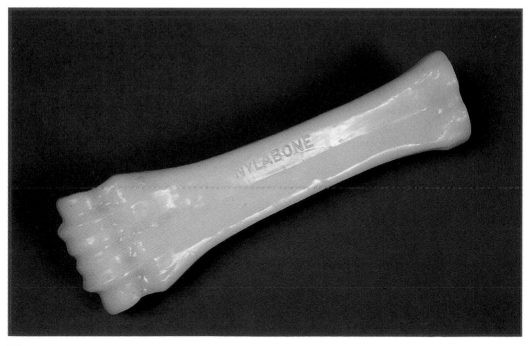

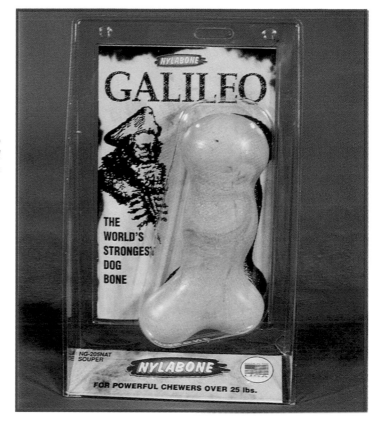

The Galileo™ is flavored to appeal to your dog and annealed so it has a relatively soft outer layer.

chewed up and eaten by dogs. At the very least, digestion is interrupted; at worst, the dog can choke or suffer from intestinal blockage.

When a dog chews hard on a Nylabone®, little bristle-like projections appear on the surface of the bone. These help to clean the dog's teeth and add to the gum-massaging. Given the chemistry of the nylon, the bristle can pass through the dog's intestinal tract without effect. Since nylon is inert, no microorganism can grow on it, and it can be washed in soap and water or sterilized in boiling water or in an autoclave.

For the sake of your dog, his teeth and your own peace of mind, provide your dog with Nylabones®. They have 100 variations from which to choose.

FIGHTING FLEAS

Fleas are very mobile and may be red, black, or brown in color. The adults suck the blood of the host, while the larvae feed on the feces of the adults, which is rich in blood. Flea "dirt" may be seen on the pup as very tiny clusters of blackish specks that look like freshly ground pepper. The eggs of fleas may be laid on the puppy, though they are more commonly laid off the host in a favorable place, such as the bedding. They normally hatch in 4 to 21 days, depending on the temperature, but they can survive for up to 18 months if temperature conditions are not favorable. The larvae are maggot-like and molt a couple of times before forming pupae, which can survive long periods until the temperature, or the vibration of a nearby host, causes them to emerge and jump on a host.

There are a number of effective treatments available, and you should discuss them with your veterinarian, then follow all instructions for the one you choose. Any treatment will involve a product for your puppy or dog and one for the environment, and will require diligence on your part to treat all areas and thoroughly clean your home and yard until the infestation is eradicated.

THE TROUBLE WITH TICKS

Ticks are arthropods of the spider family, which means they have eight legs (though the larvae have six). They bury their headparts into the host and gorge on its blood. They are easily seen as small grain-like creatures sticking out from the skin. They are often picked up when dogs play in fields, but may also arrive in your yard via wild animals—even birds—or stray cats and dogs. Some ticks are species-specific, others are more adaptable and will host on many species.

The cat flea is the most common flea of dogs. It starts feeding soon after it makes contact with the dog.

The deer tick is the most common carrier of Lyme disease. Photo courtesy of Virbac Laboratories, Inc., Fort Worth, Texas.

The most troublesome type of tick is the deer tick, which spreads the deadly Lyme disease that can cripple a dog (or a person). Deer ticks are tiny and very hard to detect. Often, by the time they're big enough to notice, they've been feeding on the dog for a few days—long enough to do their damage. Lyme disease was named for the area of the United States in which it was first detected—Lyme, Connecticut— but has now been diagnosed in almost all parts of the U.S. Your veterinarian can advise you of the danger to your dog(s) in your area, and may suggest your dog be vaccinated for Lyme. Always go over your dog with a fine-toothed flea comb when you come in from walking through any area that may harbor deer ticks, and if your dog is acting unusually sluggish or sore, seek veterinary advice.

Attempts to pull a tick free will invariably leave the headpart in the pup, where it will die and cause an infected wound or abscess. The best way to remove ticks is to dab a strong saline solution, iodine, or alcohol on them. This will numb them, causing them to loosen their hold, at which time they can be removed with forceps. The wound can then be cleaned and covered with an antiseptic ointment. If ticks are common in your area, consult with your vet for a suitable pesticide to be used in kennels, on bedding, and on the puppy or dog.

INSECTS AND OTHER OUTDOOR DANGERS

There are many biting insects, such as mosquitoes, that can cause discomfort to a puppy. Many diseases are transmitted by the males of these species.

A pup can easily get a grass seed or thorn lodged between his pads or in the folds of his ears. These may go unnoticed until an abscess forms.

This is where your daily check of the puppy or dog will do a world of good. If your puppy has been playing in long grass or places where there may be thorns, pine needles, wild animals, or parasites, the check-up is a wise precaution.

SKIN DISORDERS

Apart from problems associated with lesions created by biting pests, a puppy may fall foul to a number of other skin disorders. Examples are ringworm, mange, and eczema. Ringworm is not caused by a worm, but is a fungal infection. It manifests itself as a sore-looking bald circle. If your puppy should have any form of bald patches, let your veterinarian check him over; a microscopic examination can confirm the condition. Many old remedies for ringworm exist, such as iodine, carbolic acid, formalin, and other tinctures, but modern drugs are superior.

After a romp outdoors, be sure to check your Whippet's coat for parasites like fleas and ticks.

Fungal infections can be very difficult to treat, and even more difficult to eradicate, because of the spores. These can withstand most treatments, other than burning, which is the best thing to do with bedding once the condition has been confirmed.

Mange is a general term that can be applied to many skin conditions where the hair falls out and a flaky crust develops and falls away.

Often, dogs will scratch themselves, and this invariably is worse than the original condition, for it opens lesions that are then subject to viral, fungal, or parasitic attack. The cause of the problem can be various species of mites. These either live on skin debris and the hair follicles, which they destroy, or they bury themselves just beneath the skin and feed on the tissue. Applying general remedies from pet stores is not recommended because it is essential to identify the type of mange before a specific treatment is effective.

Eczema is another non-specific term applied to many skin disorders. The condition can be brought about in many ways. Sunburn, chemicals, allergies to foods, drugs, pollens, and even stress can all produce a deterioration of the skin and coat. Given the range of causal factors, treatment can be difficult because the problem is one of identification. It is a case of taking each possibility at a time and trying to correctly diagnose the matter. If the cause is of a dietary nature then you must remove one item at a time in order to find out if the dog is allergic to a given food. It could, of course, be the lack of a nutrient that is the problem, so if the condition persists, you should consult your veterinarian.

INTERNAL DISORDERS

It cannot be overstressed that it is very foolish to attempt to diagnose an internal disorder without the advice of a veterinarian. Take a relatively common problem such as diarrhea. It might be caused by nothing more serious than the puppy hogging a lot of food or eating something that it has never previously eaten. Conversely, it could be the first indication of a potentially fatal disease. It's up to your veterinarian to make the correct diagnosis.

The following symptoms, especially if they accompany each other or are progressively added to earlier symptoms, mean you should visit the veterinarian right away:

Continual vomiting. All dogs vomit from time to time and this is not necessarily a sign of illness. They will eat grass to induce vomiting. It is a natural cleansing process common to many carnivores. However, continued vomiting is a clear sign of a problem. It may be a blockage in the pup's intestinal tract, it may be induced by worms, or it could be due to any number of diseases.

Diarrhea. This, too, may be nothing more than a temporary condition due to many factors. Even a change of home can induce diarrhea, because this often stresses the pup, and invariably there is some change in the diet. If it persists more than 48 hours then something is amiss. If blood is seen in the feces, waste no time at all in taking the dog to the vet.

Running eyes and/or nose. A pup might have a chill and this will cause the eyes and nose to weep. Again, this should quickly clear up if the puppy is placed in a warm environment and away from any drafts. If it does not, and especially if a mucous discharge is seen, then the pup has an illness that must be diagnosed.

Coughing. Prolonged coughing is a sign of a problem, usually of a respiratory nature.

Wheezing. If the pup has difficulty breathing and makes a wheezing sound when breathing, then something is wrong.

Cries when attempting to defecate or urinate. This might only be a minor problem due to the hard state of the feces, but it could be more serious, especially if the pup cries when urinating.

Cries when touched. Obviously, if you do not handle a puppy with care he might yelp. However, if he cries even when lifted gently, then he has an internal problem that becomes apparent when pressure is applied to a given area of the body. Clearly, this must be diagnosed.

Refuses food. Generally, puppies and dogs are greedy creatures when it comes to feeding time. Some might be more fussy, but none should refuse more than one meal. If they go for a number of hours without showing any interest in their food, then something is not as it should be.

General listlessness. All puppies have their off days when they do not seem their usual cheeky, mischievous selves. If this condition persists for more than two days then there is little doubt of a problem. They may not show any of the signs listed, other than perhaps a reduced interest in their food. There are many diseases that can develop internally without displaying obvious clinical signs. Blood, fecal, and other tests are needed in order to identify the disorder before it reaches an advanced state that may not be treatable.

WORMS

There are many species of worms, and a number of these live in the tissues of dogs and most other animals. Many create no problem at all, so you are not even aware they exist. Others can be tolerated in small levels, but become a major problem if they number more than a few. The most common types seen in dogs are roundworms and tapeworms. While roundworms are the greater problem, tapeworms require an intermediate host so are more easily eradicated.

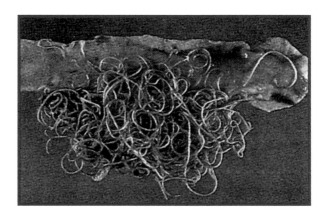

Roundworms are spaghetti-like worms that cause a pot-bellied appearance and dull coat, along with more severe symptoms, such as diarrhea and vomiting. Photo courtesy of Merck AgVet.

Roundworms of the species *Toxocara canis* infest the dog. They may grow to a length of 8 inches (20 cm) and look like strings of spaghetti. The worms feed on the digesting food in the pup's intestines. In chronic cases the puppy will become pot-bellied, have diarrhea, and will vomit. Eventually, he will stop eating, having passed through the stage when he always seems hungry. The worms lay eggs in the puppy and these pass out in his feces. They are then either ingested by the pup, or they are eaten by mice, rats, or beetles. These may then be eaten by the puppy and the life cycle is complete.

Larval worms can migrate to the womb of a pregnant bitch, or to her mammary glands, and this is how they pass to the puppy. The pregnant bitch can be wormed, which will help. The pups can, and should,

Whipworms are hard to find unless you strain your dog's feces, and this is best left to a veterinarian. Pictured here are adult whipworms.

be wormed when they are about two weeks old. Repeat worming every 10 to 14 days and the parasites should be removed. Worms can be extremely dangerous to young puppies, so you should be sure the pup is wormed as a matter of routine.

Tapeworms can be seen as tiny rice-like eggs sticking to the puppy's or dog's anus. They are less destructive, but still undesirable. The eggs are eaten by mice, fleas, rabbits, and other animals that serve as intermediate hosts. They develop into a larval stage and the host must be eaten by the dog in order to complete the chain. Your vet will supply a suitable remedy if tapeworms are seen or suspected. There are other worms, such as hookworms and whipworms, that are also blood suckers. They will make a pup anemic, and blood might be seen in the feces, which can be examined by the vet to confirm their presence. Cleanliness in all matters is the best preventative measure for all worms.

Heartworm infestation in dogs is passed by mosquitoes but can be prevented by a monthly (or daily) treatment that is given orally. Talk to your vet about the risk of heartworm in your area.

BLOAT (GASTRIC DILATATION)

This condition has proved fatal in many dogs, especially large and deep-chested breeds, such as the Weimaraner and the Great Dane. However, any dog can get bloat. It is caused by swallowing air during exercise, food/water gulping or another strenuous task. As many believe, it is not the result of flatulence. The stomach of an affected dog twists, disallowing food and blood flow and resulting in harmful toxins being released into the bloodstream. Death can easily follow if the condition goes undetected.

The best preventative measure is not to feed large meals or exercise your puppy or dog immediately after he has eaten. Veterinarians recommend feeding three smaller meals per day in an elevated feeding rack, adding water to dry food to prevent gulping, and not offering water during mealtimes.

VACCINATIONS

Every puppy, purebred or mixed breed, should be vaccinated against the major canine diseases. These are distemper, leptospirosis, hepatitis, and canine parvovirus. Your puppy may have received a temporary vaccination against distemper before you purchased him, but be sure to ask the breeder to be sure.

The age at which vaccinations are given can vary, but will usually be when the pup is 8 to 12 weeks old. By this time any protection given to the pup by antibodies received from his mother via her initial milk feeds will be losing their strength.

The puppy's immune system works on the basis that the white blood cells engulf and render harmless

Rely on your veterinarian for the most effectual vaccination schedule for your Whippet puppy.

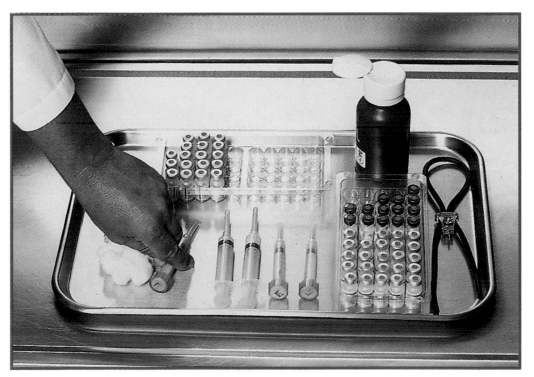

attacking bacteria. However, they must first recognize a potential enemy.

Vaccines are either dead bacteria or they are live, but in very small doses. Either type prompts the pup's defense system to attack them. When a large attack then comes (if it does), the immune system recognizes it and massive numbers of lymphocytes (white blood corpuscles) are mobilized to counter the attack. However, the ability of the cells to recognize these dangerous viruses can diminish over a period of time. It is therefore useful to provide annual reminders about the nature of the enemy. This is done by means of booster injections that keep the immune system on its alert. Immunization is not 100-percent guaranteed to be successful, but is very close. Certainly it is better than giving the puppy no protection.

Dogs are subject to other viral attacks, and if these are of a high-risk factor in your area, then your vet will suggest you have the puppy vaccinated against these as well.

Your puppy or dog should also be vaccinated against the deadly rabies virus. In fact, in many places it is illegal for your dog not to be vaccinated. This is to protect your dog, your family, and the rest of the animal population from this deadly virus that infects the nervous system and causes dementia and death.

ACCIDENTS

All puppies will get their share of bumps and bruises due to the rather energetic way they play. These will usually heal themselves over a few days. Small cuts should be bathed with a suitable disinfectant and then smeared with an antiseptic ointment. If a cut looks more serious, then stem the flow of blood with a towel or makeshift tourniquet and rush the pup to the veterinarian. Never apply so much pressure to the wound that it might restrict the flow of blood to the limb.

In the case of burns you should apply cold water or an ice pack to the surface. If the burn was due to a chemical, then this must be washed away with copious amounts of water. Apply petroleum jelly, or any vegetable oil, to the burn. Trim away the hair if need be. Wrap the dog in a blanket and rush him to the vet. The pup may go into shock, depending on the severity of the burn, and this will result in a lowered blood pressure, which is dangerous and the reason the pup must receive immediate veterinary attention.

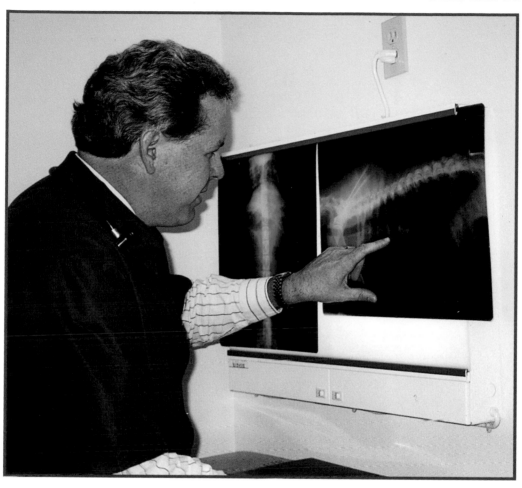

It is a good idea to x-ray the chest and abdomen on any dog hit by a car.

If a broken limb is suspected then try to keep the animal as still as possible. Wrap your pup or dog in a blanket to restrict movement and get him to the veterinarian as soon as possible. Do not move the dog's head so it is tilting backward, as this might result in blood entering the lungs.

Do not let your pup jump up and down from heights, as this can cause considerable shock to the joints. Like all youngsters, puppies do not know when enough is enough, so you must do all their thinking for them.

Provided you apply strict hygiene to all aspects of raising your puppy, and you make daily checks on his physical state, you have done as much as you can to safeguard him during his most vulnerable period. Routine visits to your veterinarian are also recommended, especially while the puppy is under one year of age. The vet may notice something that did not seem important to you.

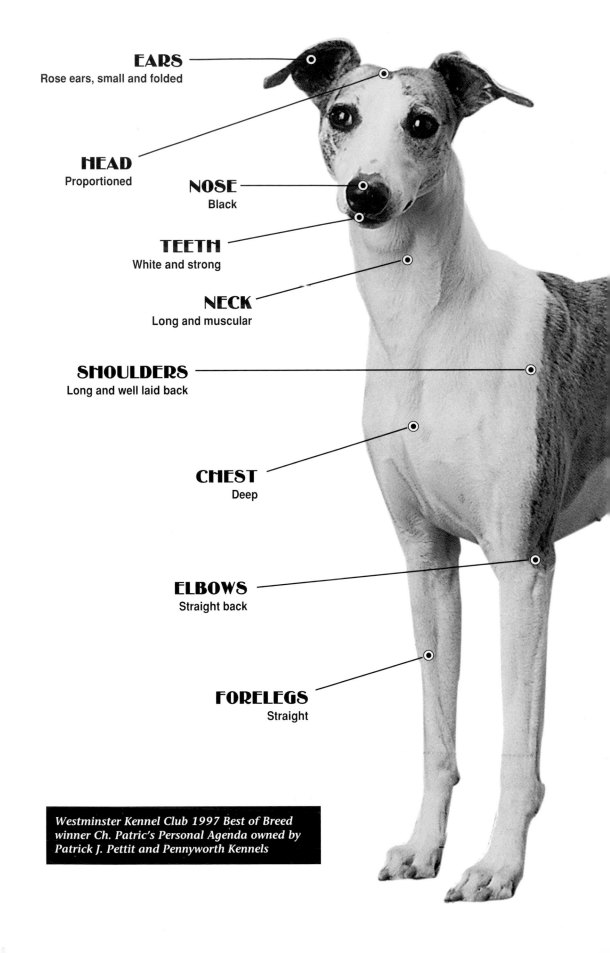

EARS
Rose ears, small and folded

HEAD
Proportioned

NOSE
Black

TEETH
White and strong

NECK
Long and muscular

SHOULDERS
Long and well laid back

CHEST
Deep

ELBOWS
Straight back

FORELEGS
Straight

Westminster Kennel Club 1997 Best of Breed winner Ch. Patric's Personal Agenda owned by Patrick J. Pettit and Pennyworth Kennels